S.B Mukerjee

Elements of Jurisprudence

Being the Substance of a Few Lectures Based on Austin's Principles of

Jurisprudence

S.B Mukerjee

Elements of Jurisprudence
Being the Substance of a Few Lectures Based on Austin's Principles of Jurisprudence

ISBN/EAN: 9783337178949

Printed in Europe, USA, Canada, Australia, Japan

Cover: Foto ©Suzi / pixelio.de

More available books at **www.hansebooks.com**

ELEMENTS OF JURISPRUDENCE

BEING

The substance of a few lectures based on Austin's Principles of
Jurisprudence, delivered to the law class of the Punjab
University College

BY

S. B. MUKERJEE, M. A. & B. L.,

Assistant Professor, Lahore Govt. College.

—◦o§o◦—

Lahore:

PRINTED AT THE CIVIL AND MILITARY GAZETTE PRESS.

1877

Jurisprudence is defined as the science of positive laws, established by the political superiors of a community. The positive laws are emphatically called the *laws* for reasons to be hereafter stated. The positive laws of a particular community collected together form what is called a body or system of law, and the science with reference to them is Particular or National Jurisprudence. When the principles, notions and distinctions common to various mature systems of positive laws obtaining in different civilised communities are regarded by themselves, the subject forms an extensive science called the science of General Jurisprudence. Particular Jurisprudence then is the exposition of the general principles of the body of laws obtaining in a community, while General Jurisprudence is the exposition and description of general principles and ends of law abstracted from the positive systems of all civilised communities. With the goodness or badness of laws Jurisprudence has no direct concern. In this respect it differs from Ethics or the science of morals. Ethics has for its object the law as it should be rather than law as it is. It determines the list of principles according to which all positive laws must be fashioned in order to merit approbation. In other words, Ethics lays down and investigates principles of general morality which are sometimes called the laws of God, known to us by a peculiar moral sense or conscience, or by a notion of general utility, or by the various other tests which divide the opinion of philosophers. Ethics is thus by a far wider subject than Jurisprudence, for it comprehends the whole range of morality, and treats of virtue and vice; whereas Jurisprudence regards chiefly the duties and rights considered as a rule of external conduct of man as a social being and responsible to society.

The particular department of Ethics which relate specially to positive laws is denominated the science of politics or legislation. In as much as the knowledge of what ought to be supposes a knowledge of what is, legislation pre-supposes Jurisprudence ; but Jurisprudence is independent of legislation, for it is clear that we can know what law is, without knowing what it should be.

Although Jurisprudence is thus an entirely different science from legislation, the former can scarcely be treated apart from the latter. For in explaining the origin and mechanism of a positive law, the student must understand the purpose and considerations which lead to its establishment. Unless the cause of laws and of the rights and obligations they create, is well understood, the laws themselves are unintelligible. Thus the Hindu law of inheritance cannot be mastered unless the peculiar institution of the shradhs which form its basis are preciously studied. The existing revenue systems of India can never be thoroughly understood without an insight into the views of the legislators who established them. Notwithstanding this close relation between the subjects, their respective provinces should be clearly distinguished, and an occasional digression into the subject of Legislation will consequently be necessary in order to expound the positive law so that the two may not be confounded.

The advantage of studying the science of Jurisprudence cannot be over-rated. It is admitted on all hands that a general knowledge of the positive laws under which we live is absolutely necessary for our safe conduct in all the various dealings between man and man, without which Society could not exist for a moment. From notions of expediency, our ignorance of law is never admitted as an excuse. In the Indian Penal Code it is distinctly stated that a mistake in fact might be advanced in some cases of offence as an excuse, or at least as a palliation, but a mistake in law never. Law therefore presumes a knowledge of law in all subjects of the state. How far this presumption is correct, this is not the place to consider. But since such is the law under which we live, it behoves us all to have a knowledge of the leading laws of our community. In order to this purpose a well grounded knowledge of the principles of Jurisprudence is of the utmost importance. To the student who begins the study of positive law without some previous acquaintance with the *rationale* of law in general, it may appear as an assemblage of arbitrary and unconnected rules. A previous knowledge however of the general principles of Jurisprudence, with a map of the law distinctly impressed upon his mind, will enable him to obtain a clear conception of it with comparative ease and rapidity. The laws that appeared before incoherent will become parts of a systematic and consistent whole. He will then understand the relations of the various parts to one another, the dependence of the particular facts on general principles in their various gradations and the general harmony running through the whole. The mental discipline which such a study engenders will be invaluable. It will enable the student to master with ease any foreign system of law, especially English law, to which he may direct his attention. Living as we do under a system of law for the most part framed by Englishmen generally from English model, some knowledge of the English systems is indispensable to the clear comprehension of our own. Our own system is still acknowledged to be imperfect because it is recent : there remain gaps in every direction to be filled up only gradually and in the course of time. Thus we have not as yet any recognized law of mortgage, torts, and several others affecting our daily relations ; whenever any case occurs where the existing law of our country is inapplicable or wanting. Judges in India are authorised to follow the English law. In fact, so numerous are the principles of English law transplanted into our own, that our knowledge of law is hardly complete without some acquaintance of English law. Now a previous study of the general principles of Jurisprudence facilitates more than anything else the study of English law, for a lawyer who has mastered the Jurisprudence of his own country has implicitly mastered most of the substance of the law which obtains in any other country, so great is the affinity between them. Even the law of a country with which we have no direct concern is not without its use. For apart from all other considerations the knowledge of a foreign system only can direct our attention to the excellencies or defects in our own. And as has been stated the study of Jurisprudence is the safest and most convenient way of attaining the ends above indicated, the time and labor bestowed upon it will not be wasted in an unprofitable undertaking.

The word *Law* is an ambiguous term, admitting of various shades of meaning. The word as generally used embraces all the different kinds of laws which we find operating in nature. But strictly speaking, law is a rule of conduct laid down for the guidance of an intelligent being by another intelligent being having a power over him.

Some of these laws are laws properly so called, and others are called laws improperly, merely from a notion of analogy or resemblance subsisting between the former and latter. Thus for example, the generalisation of Newton that every particle in the universe attracts every other particle with a force depending upon their masses and the distance between them, is called the *law* of gravitation. Kepler's proposition that the planets move in ellipses with the sun in a focus, is called the *law* of planetary motion. It is needless to remark that these laws as they are called, differ very widely from laws which form the matter of Jurisprudence; *for example*, a law which ordains that all contracts of a certain description shall be enforced or that a person committing murder shall be hanged. The analogy or resemblance by which both of these different things are denominated by the same name of laws, is a certain uniformity in their process.

Law generally speaking is therfore a declaration of uniformity and a relation of cause and effect. This analogy or resemblance may or may not be very close, *e. g.* a rule established and enforced by a mere opinion or sentiment of an indeterminate body of men in a society, is called law from a very close resemblance to the law which is properly so called; for there is intelligence in the body which imposes, and the body upon which it is imposed. But the fact that "fire burns anything thrown into it" is a law only from a remote or trifling analogy. These latter laws, which are also called physical or natural laws, are called laws from a mere caprice of fancy. They are not properly laws as are dealt with in Jurisprudence because they are not addressed to sentient beings, and therefore there is no choice by which the law might be obeyed or disobeyed.

Excluding then physical laws, all other laws are defined to be commands issued by superiors to inferiors. But what is a command? An expression or intimation of a wish, is a command. This intimation must be made by a person having the power to enforce the command; for an intimation of wish without power to enforce it, is not a command, but becomes a *request.* Also there must be purpose on the part of the commander to enforce the command, for otherwise the form of the expression may be that of a command, but the substance of it is simply a request.

Thus the word command is not synonymous with law, but has a wider signification. A command is particular or general, that is it may be addressed to

one individual, or to many individuals ; or again, it may
be to do or forbear from doing a particular act or a class of
acts.   Thus if an order is given to a servant to do a particular act on a particular day, the order is merely specific; but if the order be to do that act regularly from day
to day, the order becomes general.

A particular command is not a law or rule.   No
doubt an occasional command issued by a monarch or
a soverign body is very frequently called a law.   But
it is better to distinguish the two cases and appropriate
the word law only to the commands which are general
in their nature.

Hence all laws, properly so called are defined to be
commands which oblige generally to acts or forbearances
of a class, and are addressed to one or a number of individuals.

Some writers attempted to define law as a command issued from a superior to an inferior.   But a command issued by a superior is a tautological expression.
The word *Command* implies superiority, for superiority is
only the power of enforcing compliance with a wish ; and
the intimation of the wish with the power and purpose
of enforcing it, is a constituent element of command.
Hence "Laws emenate from superiors" is an identical
proposition; for the meaning which it imports is really
contained in the subject.

All laws enjoin either action or omission ; that is,
they command either to do an act, or refrain from doing
an act.   Omissions may be as much illegal as actions.
Most offences can be committed either by doing an act
or by omitting to do an act.   For instance murder can be
committed either directly by a sword, or omitting to give
food to one to whom it should be given.   In these
cases omission leads to an offence.   But in those cases

where a positive duty is imposed, as for example, an injunction to perform contracts, omission means the violation of the order and then it is itself illegal.

If the matter is closely examined, and distinction is made between the laws which are rightly so called, from the laws which are improperly so called, we shall find that a law proper must have the following essential elements : (1). It is a command—command issuing from a determinate source or a determinate authority. In other words, the intimation of wish constituting the command, must proceed from a determinate rational being, or a determinate rational collective body. Unless a body be precisely determinate or certain, it cannot signify a wish or command. A body is said to be indeterminate when the persons composing the body cannot be indicated or pointed out. Thus the members of a trading firm or company form a definite body. But a section of Englishmen averse to native improvement, may be said to be an indeterminate body; for it is impossible to point out any particular Englishman holding such an opinion. So long as these remain an indeterminate body, they are not able to pursue a definite course, or intimate a definite wish. But it must be recollected that a definite body may at any moment be formed out of an indeterminate body ; and the body thus formed will then of course possess all the functions of acting in a corporate capacity, and be able to promulgate rules or commands for the guidance of others, which will be properly called laws.

(2). Every such command must have a sanction annexed to it. That is, a punishment attendant upon the infringement of the command is annexed for the purpose of enforcing obedience. The nature of the sanctions will be explained further on. (3). There must be always some right conferred or duty imposed by the command.

If we now try by the above tests, we find that all laws properly so called, together with certain others which are improperly called laws, can be divided into two classes, (1) Laws set by God to men, (2) laws set by men to men. The first are called Divine laws, the laws of nature or the natural laws. The second class of laws, are necessarily imperfect. The first is a test by which the second must be examined; that is, laws of men to men are considered perfect only when they conform to the laws of God.

The laws of God are evidently laws rightly so called; for they are commands either express or tacit, emanating from a definite intelligent source, and have for their object the guidance of intelligent rational beings. The violations of these laws are called Sins, and the evils or punishment annexed to them are various religious penalties, including the punishment in a future state.

The laws of men to men are subdivided into two classes :

(1) Positive law (2) Positive morality. Positive laws are rules of conduct prescribed by political superiors of a community. Their immediate authors may be of three kinds : (a) Monarchs or sovereign bodies, as supreme political superiors. (b) Subordinate political superiors exercising authority from delegation. (c) Private men having authority to command in pursuance of legal rights, as guardians regulating the conduct of their wards.

Positive morality, otherwise called positive moral rules, are those which are not thus imposed by political superiors ; and in this, they differ from positive laws. They are of two sorts, some are laws properly so called, others are called laws by reason of resemblance or analogy. The former are laws properly so called, for they conform to the tests previously stated, while the latter do not

Positive moral rules which are properly called laws, may be referred to these three heads :

(1.) Those that are set by men living in a state of nature or anarchy. Here as there is no recognized government, the person issuing the command cannot be a *political* superior. Neither can he have any legal right to issue a command. But as he is a determinate and intelligent author of the command, guiding the conduct of one or more intelligent beings by means of sanctions of his own, his command is properly called law, although it differs materially from positive law.

(2.) Those that are imposed by sovereigns, but not in their character of political superiors, upon sovereigns of other political societies. Since no supreme government is in a state of subjection to another, a law cannot be set by one sovereign to another in the character of political superior. Nor can it be in pursuance of any legal right ; for legal rights are conferred by law, and only to political inferiors. Hence a command issued by one sovereign power to another, although not positive law, is still law properly so called, and falls under the head of positive morality.

(3.) Those that are imposed by subjects as private persons, not in pursuance of any legal right ; as a father issuing an imperative law to his child, or a master to his servant. If he imposes such law in pursuance of a legal right, his law becomes positive law ; otherwise it is simply a rule of positive morality : for a child or a servant is not bound to follow the command by sanction of the political sovereign of the community. But nevertheless, it is a law properly so called, in as much as it conforms to the three tests before enumerated.

The second class of positive morality, namely those that are not laws properly so called, or are called so from a notion of resemblance or analogy, are chiefly the laws set or imposed by general opinion ; that is the opinion of an indeterminate body of men. We have seen before that an indeterminate body of men is incapable of issuing a command. Nevertheless, we may be sure that a particular opinion regarding a particular conduct is entertained by a section or majority of persons in a society, and that a conduct contrary to such opinion will be resented or meet with certain painful consequences. These opinions prevail in society by habit, mode of thought, and in short by the general tone of morality in the country. For example, the maxim of Hindu morality forbids the remarriage of widows. Although this maxim exists only as a general opinion, its stringency is remarkable. In the very face of a positive law legalising it, it persistently maintains its ground, and the society visits with condign punishment the man who dares to disobey it.

Examples of this class of positive morality are also found in what are called laws of honor, laws of fashion, laws of etiquette, and so forth. The international law, or the rules of international morality also belong to this class. These rules and maxims are based on general principles of utility, regulating the intercourse of one nation with another. In other words, they have regard to the conduct of sovereigns towards one another, for sovereigns are representatives of their respective nations. The regulation of trade and commerce, the declaration of war and peace and the like, are matters of international law. It is evident they are never promulgated by any definite act of man, but rest simply upon a general opinion of mankind for their usefulness and validity. Hence they are not laws in the proper acceptation of the term, much less positive laws. They have received the name of laws only from a greater or less resemblance they bear to those that are properly called laws. These analogies may be briefly stated thus :

(1.) The indeterminate body holding a general opinion feels that a particular conduct must be pursued or forborne just as if that conduct were imposed by law properly so called.

(2.) In the case of a law imposed by general opinion, as in that of a law proper, there are equal or similar chances of undergoing some kind of evil as a consequence of violating the law. In other words, both of these are followed by some sort of sanction.

(3.) In both of these cases, the conduct to be pursued has a uniformity or steadiness of character. In fact the perception of this uniformity of sequence is the chief justification of the use of the term law to facts otherwise quite dissimilar.

Here it should be noticed that when the laws of men are divided into positive law and positive morality, the word *positive* simply signifies that such a law or such a morality holds in the country, without any consideration of its being good or bad. The goodness or badness of a law has nothing to do with its being a law. So it is not rare, that we find laws and morality which are not only indifferent, but absolutely repugnant to all notions of justice and propriety.

Positive laws only, and some laws improperly so called which will presently be mentioned, form appropriate matters of jurisprudence; and the business of a lawyer is confined to the knowledge of what law is, rather than what law should be. He expounds the meanings of positive law, reconciles one portion with another, and applies general principles to particular cases. Whether the particular law which he is called upon to expound is good or bad, that is whether it conforms to general utility or the purpose for which it is promulgated, is a separate question, and belongs to the province of legislation. This is a department of ethical science to be principally studied by the legislators or the members of our legislative councils. The lawyer only deals with law as it exists.

There are however some laws not properly so called, which nevertheless, form appropriate matters of jurisprudence. These are :

(1.) Declaratory laws, or laws promulgated by legislature to explain positive laws. They are not commands, for they do not establish new duties, but only explain and declare the duties already established.

(2.) Laws abrogating or repealing existing positive laws. In so far as they release from existing duties, they are not commands, but the revocation of former cammands.

It was formerly a question whether an original law revives in those cases when a law repealing the same, is itself repealed. In India the matter has been finally settled by a definite act of legislature, that the former law does not revive unless expressly provided.

(3.) Imperfect laws or laws of imperfect obligation, that is, laws wanting legal sanction. When the legislature imposes a duty, but either by design or oversight, neglects to lay down the penalty of violating it, the law falls under this head. In India or England however, such a law is nowhere found. For where the legislature has omitted to mention the sanction, the tribunal supplies it agreeably to the case in hand.

It may not be perhaps out of place here to notice that a law set by a party to himself is an impossibility. He simply determines to do, or omits to do a particular class of actions. Here there is no order proceeding from any body, nor any sanction to enforce obedience. Hence a routine of acts set by one's own self can be called a law only in a metaphorical sense. A mistake of this kind which is so obvious when stated, has been the source of much confusion and error. For example, it is sometimes stated that a government lies under a legal duty to obey an enactment it has passed. Nothing can be more absurd. Government may be under a religious or moral obligation to follow its own determination ; but to imagine a legal obligation would be to suppose, that the law proceeded from a higher body different from government itself. This will be further explained when the nature of an independent government is understood.

It will be seen now, that a law ordained by God, positive law and positive morality, proceeding from different sources and from different circumstances, need not be coincident. In fact, they are often found widely conflicting. Although, as a general rule, the legislator should always try to make positive law conform to Divine law, still in the absence of a distinct revelation, he has no other guide but his own abstract notion of general utility; and it is quite possible that his view is not the correct one. Hence arises that divergence between what is called Divine law, and the positive law of a country. Instances of positive law conflicting with positive morality, are not rare. The legislator may in his individual notion of utility enact a law which is quite inconsistent, nay antagonistic to some rule of positive morality in the country. Act 15 of 1856 legalising remarriage of Hindu widows, is a notable example of this kind of legislation.

But inconsistencies and antagonisms like the above are rather the exception than the rule. As a general fact the laws from these three sources coincide. But we must be careful not to confound in any particular case the true source of the law. Thus when a conduct which is approved by the law of God, or by the general opinion of the community, is made a matter of positive law, the sovereign legislature must be regarded as the true source of the law, although the lawgiver might have modelled his law on Divine law or positive morality.

We have seen above that the commander, in order that a command may be law, must have power and intention of enforcing compliance ;—in other words, he must attach positive punishment, in case his command be disobeyed. This eventual evil is called the sanction of law, or the duty imposed by the command, is said to be sanctioned. The party upon whom the duty is incumbent, is liable to incur evil consequences in case he violates the duty. The prospect of such evil enforces compliance with the command by operating upon the desires of the party commanded, for his mind is so constituted that he is naturally averse to undergo the evil with which he is threatened. The magnitude of the evil may vary widely. From a simple rebuke it may rise to the loss of life and the confiscation of all worldly effects. In fact, the greater this evil and the chance of incurring it, the greater is the efficacy of command. But in order that an intimation of a wish may amount to a command, it is sufficient to annex some sort of evil whether proportionate or not. The sanction may be feeble or insufficient, but its existence is absolutely necessary to turn the wish to a command, and the conduct imposed, to a duty.

The object of every duty is an act or forbearance. When we do an act, or forbear from doing an act, the act or forbearance is the consequence of a desire in our mind. Our desires are regulated by motives. Now, what the sanction of law really does, is to furnish the party commanded with a motive, *viz.* the motive of avoiding an evil. But a man cannot be obliged or forced to desire or not to desire ; that is to say, the existence of a motive to desire does not preclude the possibility of conflicting desires. The desire of avoiding an evil may master or control, but cannot extinguish a conflicting desire which urges man to a breach of duty. Hence it is no wonder, that in spite of the most stringent sanctions, important duties and obligations are every day seen violated.

But although the desire of avoiding a sanction cannot *directly* extinguish a conflicting desire, it may do so gradually, or by association or habit. This depends upon the familiar phenomenon of habit. Objects originally pleasing become displeasing by being constantly associated with painful objects, and *vice versa*. The constant association of a wrong with the fear of incurring the evil which the law annexes to it, generates a habit of disliking the wrong for its own sake. The conflicting desire of enjoying the pleasure which the violation of a duty may bring in, gradually becomes weaker and weaker, until it is wholly extinguished by the stronger desire of avoiding the evil or sanction. This habitual fear of punishment, says Hobbes, makes men just, meaning that the fulfilment of the obligation no longer becomes an effort, but follows spontaneously. When such a state of the mind has been attained, the violation of the duty becomes an unlucky chance, and is visited on all societies with a more mitigated punishment than would otherwise be the case. In criminal courts of our country, evidence of good character in the prisoner is always admissible not only to rebut the presumption of guilt, but also to mitigate the punishment when proved. For the criminal then becomes more an object of pity than of antipathy. The reason seems to be that such a special mercy shown to the habitual regard for laws encourages a similar conduct in the whole of the community.

Sanction is then a necessary concomitant of obligation. The difference between them is simply this, that sanction is the evil to be incurred by disobedience to a command, while obligation is the liability to incur that evil.

Again sanction must be distinguished from physical or natural compulsion. From what has been said above, sanction is the compulsion upon our desires, whereas physical compulsions are compulsions upon our wills or actions. For we may be compelled to act against our desires. Physical compulsions are therefore applied directly to our body, *e. g.* when a man is locked up in a room, he cannot move out in spite of his strong desire to do so. But if you place him in a room and order him not to go out on pain of death, you simply offer him two alternatives, *viz.* either to remain in the room or suffer death, and he can take his choice. Here a motive is offered to him to govern his desire and he has the liberty to select the lesser evil.

Physical compulsion is then only a form of bodily suffering which is the ultimate basis of most obligations or duty. As a matter of fact, sanction is not always at first a bodily pain. Generally the sanction of an obligation is another obligation; thus, *c. g.* a man violates a contract, and the sanction is to pay damages. This sanction is only another obligation imposed upon him. The command to pay damages may be further sanctioned by a fine or imprisonment, and it is only in the last resort that he may be visited with a bodily suffering and pain, and there the obligation will perhaps end.

It may be observed that in order that the sanction may operate upon the desire of the party commanded to fulfil the obligation, it is necessary that two conditions must concur :

(1.) That he should actually know the law, or with proper care might have known the law, and (2) that he must know or might know with reasonable care, that the action or omission in a particular case amounts to a breach of the commandment. For the first purpose, it is proper that the command should be explicit, and the sanction distinctly stated, so that every person whom they affect may have the opportunity of knowing the law. With regard to most positive laws of our country, this is effected by publishing the laws at least three times in the Government Gazette. A knowledge of law therefore in those that can read is reasonably presumed, and if any one does not know it, he is himself to blame ; and his negligence cannot be advanced as an excuse for liability. But our legislature goes further and presumes the knowledge in every subject. This presumption notoriously false as it is,

is only justified by its expediency. To say that it is
possible for every one to know the law is manifestly false,
for not to speak of illiterate people the very best lawyers
sometimes betray an ignorance in the very law they
profess to expound. To say that his ignorance is no
excuse, because he is bound to know the law, is simply a
reasoning in a circle ; for it assigns the rule as a reason
for itself. The presumption however rests upon the solid
basis of utility. If the ignorance of law were admitted as
a ground of non-liability, it would always be alleged by
the party, and the court would be involved in questions
scarcely possible to be solved. How for instance can it
be decided that the party had not the knowledge at the
time of committing a wrong, or that he might not have
the knowledge with reasonable care on his part? For the
purpose of determining the reality and assigning the
cause of this ignorance the court will be driven to search
the whole life and history of the offender, and to enter
upon questions of fact, insoluble and interminable. Administration of justice would be next to impracticable, and
the law would be all but useless.

To the general rule that ignorance of law is no excuse, exceptions are very rare. Section 94 of the Indian
Penal Code contains an instance to the point, viz., where
a man is compelled by another to commit a crime short of
murder, by fear of instant death to himself. If he yields to
the fear of any other harm to himself, he is not excused.
But the fear of instant death is supposed to deprive him
of all free will. His act can therefore be scarcely called
his own, and the punishing of him would be as absurd
as to hang a sword that kills. He is therefore rightly
excused. In the case of infants below seven years of
age and analogous cases, the exemption from liability,
lies not upon their ignorance, but their general incapa-
city to understand the nature of law and facts.

With respect to the other requisite for sanction
to operate upon the motive of the party commanded,

viz. the knowledge of fact, it is admitted by every system of Jurisprudence as a proper ground of exemption from liability. Not that ignorance of fact differs in its character very materially from ignorance of law, but that in this case, the admission of the ground is not attended with those inconveniences previously stated. Whether the ignorance of fact really existed, and how far can it be imputed to the negligence of the party, are questions of fact that can be solved by examining into the circumstances of the case. The administration of justice would not be perplexed. Whenever such ignorance of fact is proved before the Court, it rightly forms valid excuse for the party charged with the disobedience of law ; for the sanction annexed to the law, had no operation in his case, and it would be improper to punish a man for conduct without furnishing him a motive for pursuing a different course.

It might be said that rewards as well as punishments serve as motives to conduct. Rewards however can merely persuade or allure, they can never oblige. If the law hold out some reward as an inducement to do an act, a prospective right is merely conferred, but no obligation is imposed. The man disobeying the law or command simply foregoes the reward, but incurs no positive loss. Hence it is that human legislation for the most part chooses to make laws consisting of punishment rather than rewards. And as Blackstone says, "the quiet enjoyment of our civil rights and liberties which are the sure and general consequence of our obedience to the laws, are in themselves the best and most valuable of all rewards. No state can be supposed to possess funds for rewarding every obedience to law. Besides the dread of evil is a much more forcible principle of human nature than the love of reward." Hence it is that rewards are not regarded as sanctions of law.

Every expression of law, therefore, consists of two portions, one of which consists of the duty imposed and the other lays down the sanction or the contingent evil. This vindicatory part of the law is evidently the most effectual; for it is lost labor to say *do this* or *do not do this*, unless it be also declared that this shall be the consequence of your non-compliance with my order. Hence Lord Coke rightly says that execution is the life of laws.

Sanctions are divided by Austin into three classes, corresponding to the three divisions of laws properly so called. They are (1) religious sanctions (2) legal or political sanctions and (3) moral sanctions. Religious sanctions are those that are annexed to the laws of God; that is, they are punishments by which the laws of God are enforced. They consist chiefly of peace of conscience in this world and dread of punishment in the next. The punishment imposed by the religious authorities of the country for violation of divine laws, may also perhaps be called religious sanctions, but in some cases, they derive their binding force directly from legislature, and are therefore more properly legal sanctions. Legal or political sanctions are annexed to positive laws, and are pre-eminently *the sanctions*. They are manifested by the ordinary punishments of damages, imprisonment, death, transportation and so forth. Moral sanctions are those punishments that are annexed to rules of positive morality. Thus the correction of a child by its father for disobeying his command is a moral sanction; or as in our country the violation of the rule of positive morality by re-marrying a widow or crossing the sea, is punished by the loss of caste or other social degradations.

To these three classes of sanctions, Bentham adds another which he styles physical or natural sanctions. These are the evils which a sufferer brings upon himself by an act or omission of his own, the act or omission not being a violation of the law of God or of a positive law or a law of morality. Thus if you allow a property of yours to be destroyed through your own negligence you bring upon yourself a physical or natural sanction ; that is you suffer an evil without the intervention of any law.

According to Austin, physical sanctions are not properly sanctions, but are only the general modes in which all sanctions operate upon individuals, that is, they affect the sufferers through physical or material means. Thus when an offender undergoes rigorous imprisonment for a crime, he suffers the legal sanction through his physical or bodily means. When the suffering does not proceed from the violation of a law, it cannot properly be called sanction, for the essential character of the sanction is there wanting. These physical evils have been apparently called sanctions on account of the specious analogy they bear to sanctions properly so called. For instance, they like the latter are suffered by intelligent beings through some acts or omissions, and when known beforehand would affect their conduct exactly in the same way. But since they do not follow the disobedience of a command from any intelligent being, they are simple evils and not sanctions. If every possible evil which man may suffer, and which can affect his conduct be called sanction, the import of that term would be unnecessarily and arbitarily stretched, leading to confusion and ambiguity in the treatment of the subject in hand.

Having thus distinguished the different kinds of laws from the laws which are improperly so called, and described the nature and characters of sanctions by which they are enforced, I shall direct your attention to the positive laws particularly, inasmuch as positive laws are the only laws with which a student of Jurisprudence has direct concern. Positive laws have been before defined to be the rules or commands imposed by political superiors of a community. In order, therefore, to understand the subject clearly, it would be proper in the first place to study a little the notion indicated by the terms society and political superiors. The subject is an extensive one, and requires more space for its development than this short outline. I must therefore be as brief as possible.

The origin of society is found in the very nature of man. Man is so constituted by nature that he is unable to supply his own wants, and therefore requires the intercourse and assistance of his fellowmen either for his immediate preservation or for the perfection of his being. No animal is so miserable as an isolated man. If we suppose a family living together in this state, their condition would be more disadvantageous than that of animals ; for their wants are greater than can be satisfied without external aid. The greatness of man, nay his very existence, depends upon mutual co-operation and support. There is accordingly a tendency in man's nature to form society.

Now a society is either natural or civil (political). Natural society consists of relations between father and children, husband and wife, and so forth. The law of natural society is that each member should do for others everything which their welfare requires and which he can perform without neglecting those duties which he owes to himself. There are superiors and inferiors, and therefore laws and sanctions ; but the relation of sovereign and subjects which mark the character of a political society is wanting. In fact the members may be said to live in the state of independence.

Civil or political society is the development of natural society and is more essential to man's well-being than the latter. It has a sovereign power, guiding the conduct of its members. The necessity of the civil society arises from the wants and fears of the weaker members of the community. From this you will see the futility of an argument sometimes brought forward, that the rich ought to contribute more towards the maintainance of government, as they have more to loose without it. True; but the rich are better able to protect themselves. The rich and the poor are equally interested in the preservation of society.

A social state would not exist without civil government ; for there must be a power to govern the multitude. A civil society therefore implies the introduction of a sovereign power into natural society, and the partition of mankind into separate political bodies for the purpose of government. These separate bodies might be called independent political societies or states. Blackstone defines a state to be a collective body composed of a multitude of individuals united for their convenience and safety, and intending to act together as one man. Aristotle regards it as a society of people joining together with their families and children to live well, for a perfect and independent life. The end for which a state is established is that the inhabitants may live happily.

In every political society, there are two portions, one the sovereign, and the other the subjects. The superiority which is styled sovereignty and the independent political society which sovereignty implies, are distinguished from other kinds of superiority and societies by the following characteristics :—

(a.) The bulk of a given society is in the habit of obedience to a determinate and common superior, being either one individual or a number of individuals. This individual or body of individuals, is called the sovereign, and the rest who are in the habit of obedience are the subjects. The obedience of the subjects must be habitual or permanent, and not fitful or transient ; for in that case the relation of sovereignty and subjection is not established. A weaker state may for a time be overpowered by a stronger state, and the subjects of the former may be forced to obey the commands of temporary invaders. But if obedience is only temporary and not habitual the relation of sovereignty and subjection will not exist between them. The original sovereign still retains the sovereignty, although for a time deranged, unless the disobedience become habitual. Also this habitual obedience must be rendered to a determinate common superior, or a body of superiors ; for if different portions of the subjects obey different superiors, the society is either a natural one, or is split into two or more independent political societies. Lastly, the obedience must be rendered by the generalty or bulk of the members; for otherwise, there is properly speaking no government, and the society is one in a state of nature.

(b.) The ruling individual or body of individuals must not be in the habit of obedience to a determinate human superior. For if the sovereign portion of the community be in the habit of obedience to another superior, the community is no longer independent, but like a governor of a dependent state, will be dependent upon the more powerful one. It might happen however that the opinions of the members composing the society, or of another political society with which it stands in some relation, sometimes affect the conduct of the sovereign portion of the society; but such submission to a general opinion or command from a stronger power is only occasional and temporary.

In order that the society may be independent, the sovereign portion must not, as a general rule, habitually obey any determinate human superior. For if the sovereign portion habitually obey another superior, the society is no longer independent, but becomes subordinate to the other to whom the obedience is rendered. This is precisely the position of most of the states of India under native princes.

It will be seen from the above, that the sovereign portion of the community is really an independent party, while the rest are really dependent upon, or subject to it.

So that when we say that a society is independent, what we really mean is that the sovereign portion is so.

In order therefore that a given society may form a society political and independent, the two distinguishing marks stated above must unite. In an independent political society, however, there must be a certain number of persons who will habitually render obedience to the sovereign portion. This number can not be fixed with precision, but must be considerable, *i. e.* not extremely small. For unless this be the case, the society will not be deemed political or civil, but natural.

The neglect of the above two marks of independent political society has led Bentham, Hobbes and other eminent jurists to grave errors respecting its character. Thus when Hobbes says " that a society is not a society political and independent unless it can maintain its independence against attacks from without by its own intrinsic and unaided strength," he forgets that according to this test, there are few states in the world entitled to be called independent.

The proper purpose for which a government ought to exist is the greatest possible advancement of human happiness. But the general happiness of the whole of mankind consists in the aggregate happiness of particular societies into which mankind is divided. In order therefore to accomplish this purpose, the government must labour directly and particularly to advance as far as possible the weal of the particular community over which it presides. In so doing there is seldom any fear of a conflict between the general and particular interests, for the two are inseparably connected together ; and an enlightened and intelligent patriotism will always find harmony between them. It is only the narrow views of selfish politicians which endeavour to aggrandize their own country at the expense of the rest. The means by which the common weal is attained are various, but the principal are beneficial legislation, and a good administration of justice.

It follows then that the principle of utility or the greatest possible amount of good, is the basis of that habitual obedience of the subject portion to the sovereign, which constitute political society ; whenever the people consider that the government properly discharges its function, this conviction would be their motive to obedience. If they dislike a government as faulty, their dread of an evil arising from resistance and revolution coupled with the perception of a general utility of any established government compared with the evils of anarchy, master their dislike and induce them to obey.

This perception of utility and the preference of a government however bad to anarchy, are the only general causes for the permanence of political Governments, in almost all societies. There might however be particular or specific causes for the permanence of a particular society, e g. a custom, a prejudice, or a strong military force. But this is a matter of particular history. The general principle and origin of the obedience of the subject to the sovereign can be no other than a recognition of utility.

Here it will be proper to examine briefly a proposition sometimes gravely advanced, viz., that every government arises out of and continues through the people's consent. The proposition is however ambiguous and liable to be misunderstood. If it means that a society endures because the people are governed by motives of some sort or other to obey the government, it is quite right, as has been observed before. If the people combinedly determine to resist and overturn the government by permanent disobedience, there is no government however strong that can endure for any length of time; for the permanence of the obedience of the subject portion of the community, forms its very essence. But the proposition is sometimes advanced in two very mistaken senses. The first is that whenever the people, or a majority of them, dislike the existing government, it ought to be abolished. This would be true, if all the people were intelligent and well educated, that is to say if each of them could understand the principles of political science, and form independent and rational opinions. This however is not the case anywhere in the world. There is abundant evidence in history, that ignorant people may love a government which is bad, and hate a government which is good. If then a government were to cease to exist simply because a set of ignorant people happen to dislike it from a prejudice, it would be the sacrifice of the good of the society for which it exists.

A second sense in which the proposition above stated is sometimes understood is, that every government arose out of an original covenant or an agreement between the people and the sovereign. Briefly stated the hypothesis is this : when society was first formed, the subjects entered into a contract with the sovereign, and the sovereign likewise entered into a compact with the subjects. This mutual covenant formed as it were the basis of the rules by which they were to behave towards each other. In other words, the duties of the sovereign towards the subjects and the duties of the subjects to the state, had their origin from that mutual compact. The conditions set forth in this covenant formed the fundamental rules, by which the future members of the community, i e. the sovereign and the subjects, would unite themselves into an independent political community. For this purpose mutual promises were exchanged, by which the sovereign and his successors, as well as the present and future subjects, would be bound from generation to generation, and for ever. This is in short the purport of the hypothesis, which is however open to many grave objections. A few of them are briefly these :—

(1.) It is at best an hypothesis ; for it has never been traced to an historical basis.

(2.) The hypothesis is useless, for it fails to account for the natural duties of the sovereign and subjects, which it professes to accomplish. Supposing that such a covenant

really existed, it may be asked, from what source did it
derive its binding authority? Not from any positive law,
for this would imply the existence of an imaginary
sovereign. Moreover, a sovereign cannot be legally
bound by any rule emanating from himself. It must
therefore be from the divine laws or the laws of positive
morality. But even without supposing any covenant, we
could refer these duties to the same sources. The duties
of the subjects towards the sovereign, similarly, are founded
partly upon divine laws, partly upon positive law, and
partly upon the rules of positive morality. We do not
therefore require any covenant to ascribe to them their real
authority.

(3.) The hypothesis seems to have originated in a
mistaken notion, that every duty, and every right is derived from contract. This requires no serious refutation.
Rights and duties may be derived from the laws of God,
and positive morality as well as positive laws which enforces a contract.

(4.) If we analyse the notion of a contract between
a party with another, there seem to be the following elements : (a) A promise made by one party to do or abstain
from doing a particular act, with respect to the other ; (b)
the acceptance of the promise by the other party ; (c)
the signification of this promise and acceptance by words
or signs. The promise may proceed from either party,
and the other party accepts it. It follows then that the
party promised, expects that the promise will be accomp-
lished. Hence, if we suppose an original covenant, we
must necessarily suppose that a promise was proposed
by the sovereign, to all the original subjects who accepted it. Unless there was acceptance, there could be no
covenant. But the subjects could hardly accept the
promise, unless they apprehended what it was. To suppose that the subjects understood the promise made by
the sovereign, and accepted it, would be to hold, that the
subjects one and all were already acquainted with all

the rules of political science or the fundamental principles of government. This would be absurd, even if all the original members of the society were adults and intelligent ; more so in a rude society, to be for the first time formed into a civil society. In fact, most political committees have been formed in process of time, and grown out of a barbarous and unsystematic government, to their present developed state. Consequently supreme government was not constituted by the original members entering into a covenant.

(5.) Supposing there was a covenant between the original members of the society, the subsequent members would not be bound thereby. For the parties were only bound by religious and moral duties. The perception of the general utility of a measure, changes with the development of the intellectual faculties, and the religious and moral sanctions will therefore require, that the terms of such a contract be abrogated, whenever found inconsistent with the present notions of utility.

We have seen that every independent political society consists of two portions, the sovereign and the subjects. The sovereign issues positive laws, which the subjects are bound to obey. It follows then, that these positive laws, oblige only the persons who are members of the society, for the sovereign is sovereign only over his own subjects. An apparent exception to this rule occurs, in the case of aliens or strangers residing in the community. It cannot be denied that these aliens are in a great measure bound by the positive laws of the country, in which they temporarily reside. For instance, a Chinaman or an Afghan residing in India for the purpose of trade, or holding land in it, is subject to the criminal laws of our country and to most of the civil laws. In these cases the stranger seems for certain limited purposes, to become for the time being, a member of the society, so far as his avocation in the foreign country is concerned. He becomes as it were a simultaneous member of more than one community. His membership may be either perfect or imperfect, according to the peculiar positive law of the country. For example, in some countries, a person born in the country even from alien parents would be regarded by law as a rightful subject ; while in others, he becomes only partly so, and must undergo a further process of naturalisation, in order to obtain the full privileges of a subject.

From the nature of sovereignty and independent political society, a very important principle follows : the power of the sovereign, whether a single person or a collective body in an independent political society, is incapable of legal limitation. Legal limitation means limitation by positive law, and a positive law is a command proceeding from the sovereign, which a subject is bound to obey. If we then suppose that a sovereign's power is limited by positive law, that is to say, if the sovereign is bound by a legal duty, we must say that legal duty was imposed upon him by some higher sovereign power, which is inconsistent with the supposition that the society is independent. The Governor-General of India may be subject to the orders of the Secretary of State, and the Secretary of State may in his turn be subject to the commands of Parliament, but the ultimate sovereign authority must be free from all human orders. A supreme power limited by positive law is a contradiction in terms.

We have previously seen, that when we say that a sovereign is bound by his own law, the term law is so used only metaphorically ; for no one can be said to impose a law upon himself. He merely lays down a routine as a guide for his own conduct, which he has every power to alter or abrogate, whenever he finds it necessary or convenient. He may thereby violate the law of God or of positive morality, but he cannot in any sense be said to violate a legal duty. His act may be sinful, or immoral, but not illegal. Suppose for example that our government to-day assures us, that it will favor no religion in India, and to-morrow establishes a Christian bishopric from the taxes gathered from the Hindu and Mohamedan subjects, all what we can say is, that its action is inconsistent and immoral and unconstitutional. But by so doing it has not violated any positive law.

On the same principle, the attempt of sovereigns or sovereign bodies, to bind the sovereign successors by some positive enactment, is futile. The successors are not legally bound to follow the laws laid down by their predecessors; and may abrogate them at pleasure. The very character of sovereignty, makes them independent of habitual obedience to any human commandment. Since the succeeding government is sovereign for the time being, it is the author directly or circuitously of all the positive laws then obtaining in the community. It does not abrogate a law made by its predecessor, not because it is bound to keep aloof by legal sanction, but simply because it sees no necessity for a change. Nevertheless the law of its predecessor, is law at present through the power and authority of the present supreme government. It is the tacit consent of the present sovereign to acknowledge the continuance of the law of his predecessors, that gives to it a binding force. The permanent settlement of Bengal established by Lord Cornwallis in 1793, is still the law of the land, only, through the acquiescence of the successive governors general, from a perception of its useful character as an institution. At any moment if found convenient for the welfare of the country, it may be abrogated with perfect legality, although by so doing, the government would incur the charge of a great immoral act, producing infinite discontent among the landed proprietors, and want of faith in its solemn assurances and promises, among the people at large. The regulation 1 of 1793, therefore, is properly a law of the present government, although not formally passed. Hence we perceive the truth of Hobbes' remark, that "a legislator is not he by whose authority the law was first made, but he by whose authority it continues to be law." The monarch or the aggregate body, having the sovereign power for the time being, follows a law set by himself or by his predecessor, because, he is bound religiously to follow the divine law of God, and also morally to follow the rules of positive morality, *viz.*, the principles and maxims which the bulk of the people regards with approbation. If he do not act in this way, he may be open to the charge of immorality, but he does not act illegally, for the test of legality, or illegality, is his own command or laws.

The above explanations will seem to reconcile an apparently paradoxical and immoral proposition of Hobbes, *viz.* that "no law is unjust." His meaning is, that no positive law is unjust. The test of legal justice or injustice, is the command of the soverign ; hence to say that a positive law is unjust, amounts to saying that it is unjust as tried by itself, which is absurd. The word justice sometimes conveys the meaning, that it is conformable to the principles of general utility. Using the word in that sense, the proposition that " no law is unjust " may be wrong, for we can conceive a law which conflicts with the law of God, or the principles of general utility. We should then say that the law is morally unjust. But to say that it is legally unjust would be a contradiction in terms. A similar ambiguity in the words *unjust* and *illegal*, in the Hindu law for a long time perplexed our early English administrators of justice. The Hindu law recognizes the distinction between an act which is sinful or immoral, and an act which is illegal, although the intimate intermixture of positive law with religion, does not at all times render it easy to determine the precise character of the sanction which enforces it. The sinful, immoral and illegal acts are all, alike to be avoided. But a sinful and immoral act may nevertheless be held valid, when committed ; for as the text qaintly says " a fact cannot be altered by a hundied texts." In the case, for instance, of partition of family estates, it is enjoined in the Hindu law as current in Bengal, that the father must not make unequal distribution among his sons ; but if he does so, his act is nevertheless valid. The meaning is, that the father is restrained only by a religious sanction ; but since he is the absolute proprietor of the property, there is no legal objection to his distributing it as he pleases. His action then, may be censured as religiously or morally bad, or unjust, but it is legally just, because positive law empowers him to do so.

A distinction is sometimes made between Free and Despotic Governments, but the distinction is based upon a misconception. Moreover the epithets free and despotic, as applied to government, can hardly have a distinct meaning. We have seen before that a supreme government is always free to act as it chooses, *i e.* there can be no legal restraints upon its action ; in other words every supreme government is despotic. On the other hand, every government is bound by religious and moral laws ; so that although no positive law is a bar to its action, still its free action is practically restrained, by a notion of advancing the general good, and regarding the opinion and sentiments of the subject portion of the community. Under this view, no government can be said to be either absolutely free, or despotic. The distinction between free and despotic governments, therefore, lies rather in imagination than in fact.

Sometimes, the distinction referred to, means to signify, that a free government allows to the subjects, a greater amount of political liberty, than a despotic government does, and consequently the former are happier than the latter. Now it is clear that so far as regards the power of conferring political liberties upon its subjects, every government is on the same footing. Whether it exercises that power or not is a different question.

Political liberty is liberty from legal restraints, or obligations, and the sovereign is legally free to extend or abridge it at his own pleasure. Again it does by no means follow that a greater amount of political liberty will make the people happier. Political liberty and political restraints are both useful in their way. In fact, political liberty in order to be effective must be generally coupled with political restraints. For instance, if the government confers upon me the right to enjoy a particular piece of land, every other individual must be restrained from obstructing me in the enjoyment, or else the grant of the liberty will be a sham. In short, the granting or witholding of political liberty should never be the basis of praise or blame. Political liberty is not the end for which government exists. The greatest good of the community should be its only object ; so that political liberty is good when it conduces to that end, and bad when contrary. Political liberty when improperly granted becomes more harmful than political restraint ; the greater happiness of the subjects is therefore the result of a better regulation of political liberty, and not of the mere conferring of it in abundance, as would be the character of a free government in the sense of those that make the distinction above stated.

In independent political societies as above described, several forms of Government or sovereignty are found to prevail. The ancients recognized only three forms of government, *viz.*, monarchy, aristocracy and republic, according as the sovereign power resided in one individual, a number of individuals, or in the whole community. When the objects of each were not properly carried out, they called it Tyranny, Oligarchy or Democracy, which were therefore only corrupt forms of the former. In modern times, however, various forms of Government are found in the most civilised countries. According to Blackstone, all the above mentioned three forms are found combined in England, the monarchy, the aristocracy and republic, being severally represented by the King or Queen, the Lords, and the Commons.

Austin recognizes only two forms of government, *viz :* monarchy or the government of one, and aristocracy or the government of more than one. The government of all the members composing a society, although not theoritically impossible, is never found in fact. Again aristocracy is subdivided into three classes, *viz :* Oligarchy, Aristocracy (in a limited sense) and Democracy. When the proportion of the governing number to the governed is extremely small, it is oligarchy ; if this proportion be small, but not extremely small, the government is aristocracy ; and if the proportion be large, it is democracy. But this threefold division presupposes a knowledge of the definite ratio between the governors and the governed, which is impracticable to obtain. On account of this difficulty, it would be impossible to determine whether a particular government is an oligarchy, aristocracy or democracy. Hence the only precise and rational distinction is that between the government of one and that of a number, in other words between monarchy and aristocracy.

An important distinction between monarchy and aristocracy is that in the case of monarchy, the monarch is the supreme power in whatever aspect we view him ; but in aristocracy the sovereign portion is supreme when viewed in one aspect and subject in another. Viewed in its collective capacity, it is the supreme power in the state ; but the individual members are subject to this collective body, and are bound to obey their laws. Thus, the individual members of Parliament are subject to the laws promulgated by the collective body or the Parliament.

A limited monarchy is a phrase having no distinct meaning. It can only mean that monarchical power is limited,—which is a contradiction in terms. A limited monarchy so called, is only a form of aristocracy, where the sovereign power is shared by one individual, along with others. This individual is called the monarch, for the sake of pre-eminence, precedence or rank. The Queen of England is called monarch only out of a complimentary etiquette, and the title must not be understood in a literal sense.

The functions of Government are manifold. They are usually divided into three heads, *viz :* the legislative, the executive, and the judicial. But the judicial sovereign powers are merely parts of the executive ; for judges simply execute the law framed by the legislature. Again, the distinction between legislative and executive, is far from being precise ; for in most civilised countries they are often found to reside in the same body. As an instance of this, you may refer to what are called judge-made laws or precedents. These are made by the judges, while professing to adjudicate upon a case. Whenever any law framed by the legislature is found wanting, ambiguous or uncertain, the judge while pretending to find out or interpret what is old, lays down some principle in his decision which becomes in fact a new law. The same thing can be discerned when orders are issued by the executive with regard to the mode of carrying a particular law into operation ; and these orders or rules are laws in the proper acceptation of the term.

It is not necessary to dwell upon the delegation of these functions of government in various forms. Suffice it to notice, that whether the sovereign power be possessed by one individual or shared by many, the different functions can never be carried into operation by the sovereign portion alone but ; must be delegated to representatives ; and any law or rule proceeding from this representative body has as much binding force attached to it, as if it had directly proceeded from the sovereign portion.

We have now determined the sense of the word law as used in jurisprudence, and also explained the methods by which it is enforced. It now remains to touch upon some of the usual classifications of positive law, and point out their general characteristics and differences. Of course, a complete enumeration of all the classes that have been proposed from time to time, would be beyond the purpose of this short lecture. Each classification is based upon a principle of its own, and the principles of division may be as varied as you can imagine.

Law has been divided according to the different sources from which it proceeds and the different modes in which it begins and ends ; that is, this division supposes to regard the origin of laws. Under this view, all laws have been divided into written and unwritten, otherwise called the Statutory and Common laws.

The expression *source of law* is however ambiguous. We have seen before that all law proceeds from the sovereign, either directly or implicitly ; therefore taken in its proper and large sense, the sovereign is the source of all laws. But the expression here has an artificial meaning ; the *immediate* author of a law, whether he be sovereign himself or a person acting with a delegated power, is regarded as its source or fountain. Thus the Governor General in Council is the source of the Acts passed by him. The Judges of the High Courts are the sources of the Judicial decisions which are laws for all ends and purposes.

The expression source of law also means the earliest monuments or documents from which our knowledge of law is derived. Thus the Dayabhaga or the Mitakshara may be denominated as the source of our Hindu law of inheritance.

The expressions written and unwritten laws must not be understood in their literal sense. They do not signify that a particular law was committed to writing or not. In fact, all laws which are properly so called, exist in writing. A written law is one which is established by the Supreme legislature *directly*, as an Act of Parliament or an act of the Governor General in Council. Unwritten law is not directly made by the supreme legislature of the country, although it owes its authority to the tacit consent of the sovereign, as for example a customary law established or enforced by a court of justice. The distinction between written and unwritten law has been borrowed from the ancient law of Rome, and there it had a strict grammatical meaning ; for there, a written law was one which existed in a written state at or before its origin ; while unwritten law was that which was not so. The distinction therefore was originally entirely founded upon a difference in the mode in which a law was promulged. But gradually by a process too long to be here noticed, it came to signify a distinction between the immediate sources from which law is found to emanate.

Whether a law is established immediately by the supreme legislature or by a subordinate legislature having delegated authority for the purpose, it is made either *directly, i. e.* in a legislative manner, or *obliquely, i. e.* in a judicial manner. The difference in these two modes of legislation consists in this ; that in the case of direct legislation, the immediate purpose of the author is professed to establish a rule : while in the case of indirect or oblique legislation, his purpose is not so much to establish a rule, as to decide a specific case. It may be that in his decision, he introduces a new rule or principle, which will be law for all similar cases in future ; in other words, the decision passes into precedent. But the show of legislation is avoided, and the new law is obliquely introduced disguised under the garb of constructions of an old one, which it really supersedes. A law made in the former mode is called a *statute* or a statutory law and that in the latter mode, a judicial law.

The form of expression in which a statute law is expressed is quite different from that of a judiciary law. A statute law is always expressed in general or abstract terms; or that the will of the legislature is known as soon as the words are read. But a judiciary law is nowhere expressed in general terms, but must be collected from the general reasons or grounds of particular decisons, as abstracted from their individual peculiarities or differences. The part of the decision which has reference to these peculiarities cannot serve as a law for subsequent decisions.

It sometimes happens that the language in which a statute is expressed, is ambiguous, or that it fails to convey the will of the legislator. Nevertheless the imperative form of the expression is manifest. When the terms of a statute are of doubtful import, certain general rules, called rules of interpretation, are laid down by lawyers, to determine their precise meaning. But the gist of all these rules consists in determining the scope of the statute, that is to say, the end or purpose which induced the lawgiver to make it. Of course, when the language is clear, the literal sense of the terms used must be adhered to as much as possible; but then the interpretation must be given after weighing the statute as an entire whole, so that the several parts may not cross each other. It does not lie in the power of private individuals to depart from the manifest sense of a statute. But the judges of courts having subordinate legislative power conferred upon them, sometimes modify the literal sense in a remarkable way, in order that they may carry into effect the scope of the statute. But this is not interpreting the statute. It is a process of legislative amendment, which the judge in his capacity of a subordinate legislator has the power to do, in order to correct any error into which the original lawgiver might have fallen. This application of law by extension of meaning must be carefully distinguished from the induction necessary to glean out law from a judicial decision.

Judiciary law can be made either by the supreme legislator of the state, as the Queen deciding cases with the advice of her privy Council, or by a subordinate legislator as a Judge of the High Court of judicature. With respect to the judiciary law made by the judges of a court of justice there was at one time much doubt as to its very authority as law; for it appears, that the legislative character of the judge was not fully recognised. Once admit that the judge has a delegated sovereign power to correct the law when he thinks it necessary, the matter would be clear enough. But this was not easily conceded. Even Bentham ridiculed the idea, and contemptuously styled judiciary law as *Judge made* law, thereby intimating that it has less validity and respect than statutory law.

The judges may not be expressly authorised by the legislature to make laws. But it is perfectly known to be the will of the legislature that the principles of their decision should be observed as law by the subjects, and that punishments would be inflicted for violating them. It makes no difference in the matter, if the will is implicit, or not expressed in language. In our country, the Judges of the High Courts of Judicature are expressly empowered to decide according to their own sense of justice, equity and good conscience, when they find the existing statute law of the country to be wanting or insufficient to meet the case. In other words, they are empowered to supply the deficiencies of existing laws by the principles of their decisions, which become law to all intents and purposes, until the supreme legislature thinks fit formally to legislate upon the subject. Of course, speaking precisely, the will of the supreme legislature enforcing the ground of a judicial decision, is law in this case, and the Judge's decision simply furnishes an occasion for exercising that will: but this is the character of all the laws made by a subordinate legislator.

But the enemies of judiciary law do not object to it so much upon its very authority as law, as upon the propriety and advantage of having such law at all. Their principal objections may be stated as follows :—

1   A judge making a judiciary law is less liable to public control than a legislator legislating in a direct way, and therefore a judiciary law has the greater chance of being pernicious to the interests of the subject to be governed by it.   This objection is valid in the main.   For the indeterminate form in which judiciary law is clothed makes it possible for a bad judge to cover his sinister motive more effectually than a direct legislator, whose language and purpose must be plain, thereby subjecting him to the direct censure of the people.   But this objection applies more to the capacity and honesty of the judge himself, than to the mode in which judiciary law is made.   If the individual legislator whether he be Governor-in-Council or Judge of the High Court, have the good of the people at heart, a law made in either way may be hailed with pleasure ; but if he be bent upon carrying out an interested motive of his own, there is as much danger in a judiciary law as in a statute.   The only restraint upon a legislator is as we have formerly seen, public opinion, or law of positive morality ; and there is no reason why it would act more powerfully in one case than in another.

2.   A judiciary law is at best an *ex post facto* law, that is to say, the law is made after it has been violated. Unlike statutory law which is made in anticipation of future cases, a judiciary law is not known by the subjects before its violation gives occasion for its rise.   The parties therefore cannot obey the law, when all of a sudden, they come to know from the judge that they have violated a law, and must suffer the consequence. So that although it may serve for good in future decisions, with reference to the decided case by which the

law is introduced, the parties suffer without any fault of their own.

3. Even with reference to future cases, a judiciary law is open to the very grave charges of uncertainty and vagueness. This arises from two causes, (a) the enormous bulk of decisions in which the law must be sought, (b) and the difficulty of extracting the law from the particular decision in which it lies imbedded. A man must be a very clever lawyer, if he has the tact to find out the law to meet his case from the countless volumes of law reports which grace his shelve. The bulk of the community, and even the majority of lawyers themselves, have to divine the law rather than ascertain it. The judges themselves are frequently at a loss where to find it, and hence following their own notion of justice, introduce a series of conflicting decisions, which while pampering the counsels having the ingenuity to quote them, serve to throw incalculable vexation in the path of the people who have to follow them.

Of course, it must not be supposed that were the law ever so simple, and easy of access, the people or a majority of them would be able to know it. Nothing is farther from the truth, although for the sake of convenience in the administration of justice, the first presumption of law is that every one knows the law under which he lives, or that ignorance of law shall never be admitted as an excuse for violating it. This presumption will not be true even in a restricted sense, namely that a person can know the law if he likes ; for we have just seen that it is often impossible even for a trained lawyer or a judge to know it. The ground upon which the presumption rests, is that without it, administration of justice would be next to impossible ; for in almost all cases ignorance may be pleaded, and perhaps with truth. But what makes the Statutory law more advantegeous in this respect is that it is more *knowable*, at least by the lawyers. A heap of statutory laws accumulating for years together, and built fragment by fragment, is as inconvenient and inaccessible for study and reference as judiciary law. Civilised nations have accordingly recognised the advantage and utility of codification, which is however a question of time and place; for a hasty codification, and in a community which is not ripe for it, does more harm than good. In India, a move in this direction has resulted in the codification of the entire criminal law of the country in the admirable Indian Penal Code. From that time forward the necessity of simplifying statutory and judiciary law has been felt, until Mr. Fitzjames Stephen succeeded in clearing the Augean stable of statutory laws from the commencement of the British rule to his time, by his two memorable repealing acts, and the consolidation of several important branches of law into single acts, as the Evidence Act, the Contract Act and so forth. Since then, consolidation of Indian laws is going on steadily but slowly and cautiously; and we have fair hope of obtaining in no very distant time, a complete copy of the law of our country, in as simple and narrow a compass as is possible under the circumstances. With respect to judiciary law, it was only in the last year that a measure for simplifying it was adopted in the introduction of a regular and authorised law report of the High Courts; but it still remains to be seen how far it will accomplish its purpose of obviating the uncertainty and conflicting nature inherent in judiciary law.

But with all its faults, and all these and other objections justly urged against judiciary legislation, it forms a necessary part of the jurisprudence of every country. Without judiciary law statute law must be meagre It is perhaps too much to expect from direct legislators who are but mortal men, all the provisions against the ever varying circumstances of individual contingencies, which the ingenuity of parties and lawyers can devise. The existing law of the legislators will therefore be often found to be insufficient to meet the case; and unless the judges are empowered to decide it on some principle of their own, the case will never be decided at all, or post-poned to an indefinite time until the legislator can take up the matter, and frame some law on the subject. The best defence of judiciary law is therefore that it does some justice to the subjects, while absence of it would produce endless confusion.

Custom has been sometimes regarded as one of the sour-ces of positive law. It was the opinion of Blackstone and others, that judiciary laws not founded upon statutes, are but parts of a customary law, which exists as positive law by the force of immemorial usage, and the judge does not make but declare them. But this is manifestly wrong. Custom cannot be enforced as positive law, unless the sovereign legislature or the subordinate judge annexes a political sanction to it. A custom when not thus sanctioned, is simply a rule of positive morality, and derives its binding force from the concurrent opinion of the public. The legal sanction can be annexed to it either in the legislative mode, and then it forms the ground of a statute ; or it may be annexed in the judicial mode, and then the custom turns into a judiciary law or precedent. Custom then is an occasion for the enactment of a statutory or judiciary law. To speak of custom therefore as one of the sources of law, as is sometimes done, is to use the term *source* in an extended or loose signification ; for on the same ground the cause or origin of the custom itself might be called a source of the law, and so on ad infinitum. The so called customary law is nothing but a species of judiciary law, moulded upon a pre-existing custom, proved by the parties to a suit, and accepted by the judge as a ground of his decision for doing substantial justice to them.

Custom is either general or particular, that is, it may govern a large class of men, or particular families and limited set of persons. A custom of the former kind, forming the ground of several judicial decisions, comes at last to be judicially recognized by the judges, that is, accepted without proof, as the custom of primogeniture among the territorial Chiefs and Rajahs. A custom of the latter kind must be strictly proved before it can be accepted. It must also satisfy some of the important legal requisites, in order to establish its claim for consideration. Thus it must have originated spontaneously or existed from time immemorial, and been acquiesced in by all the parties concerned without hesitation. When these characteristics combine, the legislature gives effect to it in the shape of a judicial decision. The legislature may have expressly declared that a custom when thus regularly proved, shall be taken as law even in the face of a positive law to the contrary. This is the fact in the Punjab with regard to inheritance among the Hindus and Mahomedans. There can be no question about a legitimate custom rightly enforced by the tribunals. But it is curious to observe the predilection of some judges for customs claiming any notoriety whatever. An unqualified acceptance of customs having no claim to be such, or only partially established, creates a dangerous uncertainty in positive law, which cannot be too highly reprobated.

Another mode of classifying positive law is according to the subjects about which it is conversant and the different purposes which it is intended to fulfil. The object of all law is, as we have formerly seen, to create a right in favor of some person, or to impose a duty on some person. In order therefore to understand this part of the subject, we must first examine briefly the nature of the rights and duties themselves.

Every law is a command which imposes upon the party commanded an obligation or duty. This obligation may be either to perform or to abstain from performing some definite act or class of acts. Acts and forbearances are therefore the objects and purposes of duties. Accordingly an obligation is said to be positive or negative. In order to fulfil a positive obligation, the act enjoined by the command must be performed by the obliged. In order to fulfil a negative obligation, he must forbear from performing the act prohibited. Here his action is not only needless, but inconsistent with the purpose of the obligation. Bentham calls negative obligations negative services : but the expression is scarcely correct. For if you abstain from knocking me on the head, you can hardly be said to have done me a service: you have simply forborne from doing me a mischief.

Again obligations are either relative or absolute. A relative obligation is incumbent upon one party and correlates with a right residing in another party. Thus if I am commanded to perform a contract into which I entered with a person, that person has a right to enforce the performance from me. In this case the obligation on my part implies a corresponding right in another. Again if I have a right to a piece of land, every one else is under an obligation or duty not to interfere with me. In absolute obligations, no such right is implied. All our duties towards the state, such as the payment of taxes, shewing loyalty to our sovereign, &c., belong to this head. For it would be wrong to say that the state has any *right* to enforce them. The state has evidently power to enforce them, and it does enforce them, but not owing to any right created in its favour. A right cannot be created in favour of one's own self. If the Governor General in Council passes an income tax Act, he does so simply to declare in a regular form what the determination of the state is, and not for creating a right in its favor to collect the same.

All rights therefore have corresponding duties or obligations, but all duties have not necessarily corresponding rights.

All rights reside in persons, *i.e.*, men or the aggregate of men forming a corporate body. A corporate body such as a Hindu family or a joint stock company, is in legal terms, called a *person* or fictitious person. In fact the term person has a wider meaning in law. It means any body capable of holding a right.

Some rights are rights over things or persons, and others are not so. As examples of the former, we may mention the right of a person over his land, or over his servant or ward. Of the latter, the right of a promissee to enforce the promise is an instance. Rights of the former class are *rights in rem*, *i.e.*, they avail against other persons generally, or as is otherwise expressed, avail against the world at large. For the duties which correlates with them are imposed upon persons generally. These duties are all negative, being forbearance from meddling with positive rights.

Rights which are not over persons or things are sometimes available against persons generally as *e. g.*, right in a person's good name or reputation; but others are available exclusively against some determinate person or persons, upon whom the corresponding obligation lies. Such rights are called rights *in personam*. All rights arising from contracts belong to this class, for the contracts bind no one else but the parties themselves.

But a contract must be carefully distinguished from a conveyance, for they are sometimes witnessed by the same deed or instrument. For example, a deed of sale of property represents both a contract and a conveyance; it is a contract in so far as it shows the mutual consent of the parties to sell and buy, which simply creates a right *in personam* in favor of the vendor; it is a conveyance in so far as it transfers a right over the thing sold, which is a *right in rem* from the vendor to the vendee. Again right to enforce the performance of a contract may eventually lead to the acquisition of a right over a thing, or a *right in rem*, but in itself it is not a right over a thing, and is only available against the party with whom it is concerned. Hence contract can never properly speaking,

give right to a thing. At most, it can give right to a
transfer or assignment of a thing, but before the transfer or assignment formally takes place, no right to the
thing passes to the promissee.

The distinction between right in rem, and right in personam, always a difficult distinction, may be perhaps made
clearer by an example. Take for instance the right of
the father to the custody and education of his child.
The right as against the child, is a right in personam,
for the child is under personal obligation to obey his
orders, and is subject to correction in case of disobedience.
Under this aspect, the right of the father is against the
child only, and no one else. But considered in another
aspect, the right of the father is a right in rem, availing
against the world at large ; for if the child be detained from
him, he can recover him from the detainer, whoever he
may be. In fact, a distinction lies between right *against*
the child, and right *in* the child. The latter is properly
speaking not the right of custody, but a right to the
exercise of the right *of* custody, which is a right in rem
imposing negative duties upon all others not to meddle
with it. A similar two fold aspect can be taken whenever the object of a right is a person.

Every right is either a right in rem, or a right in
personam, and must have a relative duty to correspond
with it. It is created by the sovereign power for the
benefit of the determinate party holding the right. An
absolute duty. on the other hand, has no determinate
party holding the right, for whose benefit the duty is imposed. Considered in its immediate scope it is created
for the benefit of (1) one's own self, as a self regarding duty
to forbear from committing suicide, (2) for the community at large, as are most duties comprising the
matter of criminal law, (3) of the sovereign imposing
the duty, as the payment of taxes ; and lastly (4) of
creatures other than man, as the duty of forbearing from
cruelty towards animals. But considering duty with

reference to its ultimate purposes, it is created for the benefit of the community at large. For suicide is prohibited, to preserve a useful member of society, and deter others from committing the same; so cruelty to animals is punished to preserve a spirit of benevolence tending ultimately to the good of the people at large.

That a duty is imposed for the good of the community at large, is not confined to the case of duties which are absolute. In fact all duties whether relative or absolute tend ultimately to the good of the entire community. For what is the good of the entire community, but the aggregate good of several members composing it? The breach of every duty therefore affects the whole community either directly or remotely. If the breach is of a relative duty, the person holding the corresponding right suffers immediately, and the entire community suffers indirectly; whereas, if it is the violation of an absolute duty, the entire community suffers in the first place, and every member of it suffers in consequence.

The neglect of this double view of the subject has sometimes introduced much confusion in the division of all violation of legal duties into civil injuries and crimes. This distinction is sometimes supposed to be based upon the tendency of the act to affect a particular individual or the whole community. Thus Blackstone and others define civil injuries as *private wrongs* concerning individuals only; and crimes as *public wrongs* affecting the whole community. But this can scarcely be the basis of a distinction, for we have seen that every breach of a duty affects individuals as well as the community. Every offence would therefore be both crime and civil injury. But this is evidently not the case. The Indian Penal Code which is the enumeration of the criminal laws of our country, embodies almost all the duties, the violations of which are crimes. But it is not with all of them that a civil suit for damages will lie as well.

The only rational distinction between civil injuries and crimes, is based upon the distinction between relative and absolute duties, as before explained. All offences affect individuals no doubt. But some are offences against rights residing in some definite party, who when injured, has the discretion to sue the offender and recover compensation. Others are not offences against rights, but are nevertheless violations of duties, and there the sovereign or the entire community pursues the wrong-doer and inflicts upon him punishment either corporal or pecuniary. In the former, the offence is civil injury, in the latter crime.

But the province of criminal law according to modern systems of jurisprudence, is not confined to the limits indicated by the above distinction. For even in most cases of offence against relative rights, the legislature thinks it not quite sufficient to leave the pursuit entirely to the discretion of the party whose right has been violated, but assumes the pursuit itself, thereby converting a civil injury into a crime. The motives which induce the legislature to regard a particular violation of relative duty as a crime as well, that is to say, as requiring severer punishment than a mere compensation to the injured, cannot always be understood. They vary in different countries according to the peculiar temperament of the people, and even in the same country at different times. An offence which is considered in one country a mere civil injury, redressed by compensation, may be regarded in another as a crime too, requiring corporal infliction. English people are quite satisfied with pecuniary damages for the seduction of their daughters and wives, but to a Hindu ear, such a state of the law sounds rediculous, not to say monstrous. Under the old Hindu law, compensation was frequently considered sufficient for acts which in modern times would be regarded as heinous crimes, while death was frequently inflicted for acts which are now only subjects of compensation. So under the old Roman law, the class of acts forming their criminal jurisprudence was much more extensive than ideas of modern legislation can warrant. The distinction between civil injuries and crimes, as at present obtains, is rather one of punishment or sanction by which the law is enforced, than anything in the nature of the offence itself. Hence it is also that the same offence, as an assault or defamation, is both a civil and a criminal offence ; that is to say, the injured party has the discretion to sue for damages, while the soverign reserves the power of visiting the offender with punishment.

The distinction between civil injuries and crimes (private and public wrongs, as they are also called) has been sometimes wrongly placed upon other grounds. For instance, it has been sometimes urged that the criminal intention of the wrong-doer makes his offence a crime. In most crimes, it is certainly true that the evil intention forms a very material element, in so much so that the evil intention itself when terminating in an attempt to commit an offence, is punished as a crime, even when no action follows in consequence. But it is manifestly incorrect to say that evil intention is a necessary element in every crime. You have simply to go over the catalogue of crimes in the Indian Penal Code, and mark how many there are where intention of the offender is either unnecessary or superfluous to their being considered as crime. Take for example the case of negligent driving in the street, whereby a person is injured. It would be going too far to say that the driver had any intention to injure the man, on the other hand, he might have tried his utmost to prevent the injury. Nevertheless he commits an offence, and is punished. Here, it is not his evil intention, but his negligence that constitutes his reckless driving an offence or crime.

Again, it has been stated, that the distinction between civil injury and crime lies in the *purpose* or end for which the sanction is enforced. In cases of crimes, the punishment is inflicted for the sake of preventing future offences by the same offender, as well as of warning others by an example. In the case of civil injury, the object of the sanction is redress to the party injured. Now so far as the immediate end of sanction is concerned, the above view is certainly correct. The primary end of sanction in civil injury is compensation to the sufferer, but the ultimate end is, like that in criminal offence, prevention of like offences generally. The offender has not only to make ample redress to the injured party, depriving him of every advantage he might have derived from his wrong, but is in addition saddled with the costs of the proceeding, not to mention his trouble and vexation in conducting the defence. Sometimes exemplary damages as they are called, are decreed against him, not so much for redress, as for punishment. On the whole, therefore the sanction in a civil offence has as much a tendency to prevent like offences in future, as that in a crime. The end of a sanction inflicted is not therefore the basis of the distinction between civil wrong and crime. Even if it were so, the case would not be improved much. It would not help us to determine in all cases which offence is to be regarded as a wrong and which a crime.

It would appear therefore from the above considerations, that all offences against relative duty are civil injuries, that is, a wrong is immediately known to give rise to a civil action, as soon as we know that a right has been violated. But we cannot so easily declare a wrong to be a crime as well, unless it be the violation of an absolute duty. Violation of relative duty is often noted as crime by legislature, but in order to know which violation is so regarded, we have no sure basis to fall upon, but must have recourse to the positive law of the community of which the offender is a member.

Rights and duties may also be classified from another point of view. There are some rights and duties which are created for their own sake, that is, they are created without reference to any ultimate right or duty. There are other rights and duties which arise only on the violation of some right previously existing. The first are called primary or principal rights and duties, and the latter secondary or sanctioning. To take an example : the right of personal liberty is a primary right, for it exists without reference to any other right or duty, and does not take its rise in the violation of any previously existing right or duty. All other individuals are under a relative duty not to interfere with this right. But suppose a person injures my right of personal liberty by wrongful detention or restraint, immediately a new right arises in my favor to enforce damages from the wrongdoer, who is also thereby placed under a new obligation to render me compensation. My right to enforce damages and the duty on the other side to render compensation, therefore presuppose the existence of other rights and duties, whose violation gives them occasion to arise. Again the violation of this secondary duty to render compensation may give rise to a further duty to undergo imprisonment or the like. In this way, the violation of a primary right or duty gives rise to a secondary one, which in its turn may give rise to a chain of secondary rights or duties, until it ends in one or other of those forms of bodily punishment, from which enforcement can go no further. All these subsequent secondary rights and duties are called *sanctioning*, for they are created for the better protection and enforcement of those other rights and duties whose existence they presuppose.

The division of law with respect to its subjects and purposes, means a division of it into several rights and duties with which it deals. Thus law is divided into three great parts, *viz* : (1) Primary rights with primary relative duties. (2) sanctioning rights with sanctioning relative duties. (3) absolute duties both primary and sanctioning.

The law investigating the nature of the rights and duties is called the law of things ; for the word *thing*, in the phraseology of jurisprudence, signifies the subject or object of law. Every law is therefore a law of thing, for it must deal with some right or duty. But instead of treating of a right and a duty in the abstract, it is sometimes more convenient and conducive to clearness to treat them with reference to the individual character of the holder; for the individual character of the holder very frequently modifies the nature of a right which he holds, or of a duty to which he is subject. Thus the right to dispose of one's own property, or to purchase anything at pleasure, may be treated in the abstract, and legal incidents and consequences from it pointed out or enunciated. But if the holder of the right happens to be an infant or a Hindu female, it is modified in various ways, which must therefore form exceptions to the general description of this right in the law of things. A collection of rights and duties belonging to a particular person, in a modified form on account of the peculiar position of that person, is said to form the *status* of that person. Thus the rights and duties which belong to a person on account of his peculiar position of a father, a guardian, a citizen and so forth, are said to form the status of a father, a guardian, a citizen, and so forth. The law which deals with the rights and duties forming a status, is called the law of persons, which is therefore only a portion of the law of things, but treated separately on account of convenience and simplicity.

The object of this discourse was to indicate some of the main principles of the science of jurisprudence, as well as some of the recognised modes of classification of the facts with which it deals ; and to prepare the student

for a study of the particular rights and duties with
sanctions peculiar to each. It would therefore be out-
side the scope of this elementary lecture to enter into an
exposition of those details for which the student is referred to the elaborate treatises of Austin and other
jurists, and the pursuit of which he will find neither
uninteresting nor unprofitable.

www.ingramcontent.com/pod-product-compliance
Lightning Source LLC
Chambersburg PA
CBHW031751090426
42739CB00008B/966